A FRIEND LIKE ANIAN: THE FIRST DAY OF SCHOOL
© 2020 BY MEEKA CALDWELL
ILLUSTRATED BY: CAMERON WILSON

ALL RIGHTS RESERVED SOLELY BY THE AUTHOR. THE AUTHOR GUARANTEES ALL CONTENTS ARE ORIGINAL AND DO NOT INFRINGE UPON THE LEGAL RIGHTS OF ANY OTHER PERSONS OR WORK. NO PART OF THIS BOOK MAY BE REPRODUCED IN ANY FORM WITHOUT THE PERMISSION OF THE AUTHOR. THE VIEWS EXPRESSED IN THIS BOOK ARE NOT NECESSARILY THOSE OF THE PUBLISHER.

PRINTED IN THE UNITED STATES OF AMERICA.
ISBN-13: 978-1-7362758-0-1
BROWN BABY 321 PUBLISHING
UPPER MARLBORO, MD

A FRIEND LIKE ANIAN:
THE FIRST DAY OF SCHOOL

BY MEEKA CALDWELL
ILLUSTRATED BY CAMERON WILSON

Today is an exciting day; it's the first day of school! The summer was a wonderful time, being outside and playing with friends is always so much fun. But it's time for a new adventure; It's Kindergarten for Anian!

After breakfast, the kids grab their lunch, hug Daddy, and head to the car with Mommy.

"Have a great first day!" Daddy says as he waves goodbye.

"Ok!" They all say at once, running out of the door.

As they all walk together toward the car, Aven says, "Anian, are you excited? You are going to school!"

Anian says, "No, scared."

Prix says, "It will be ok, Anian. You'll see."

They all get into the car, put on their seatbelts, and are now ready to go.

When they arrive at school, they get out of the car and head into the building. Aven and Prix wave goodbye to Mommy and Anian as they go to their class. Anian looks a little sad. Mommy says, "Anian, you will be just fine. I am going to walk with you to your class, ok?"

"Ok," Anian says, still holding Mommy's hand tightly.

Mommy and Anian walk to his class. When they get there, everyone's waiting for class to start. While they wait, the kids play and laugh and jump around with each other. Anian starts feeling nervous, grabs Mommy's leg, and whispers, "Scared."

"Anian, I want you to meet your teacher," Mommy says. Anian waits as his teacher and another person walk up to him.

"Hi Anian. My name is Ms. Maple, and I'll be your teacher this year. I'm so happy to have you in my class!" said Ms. Maple. "This nice lady next to me is Ms. Grace. If you ever need any help, just let either one of us know. If I seem busy, you can always go to Ms. Grace."

Anian has Down Syndrome, which means that he might need a little extra help sometimes. Ms. Grace is an adult called an aide, who is someone who helps children like Anian every day while they're at school.

"Hi Anian," Ms. Grace says. "It is so nice to meet you. Do you want to go play with the blocks?"

"Ok," Anian says, then he and Ms. Grace walk over to the block area.

Ms. Grace will help Anian learn new things, pay attention in class, and walk around the school safely to get to different activities.

Mommy comes over to say goodbye to Anian. "Anian, Daddy will pick you up after school. I know you will have a great day," Mommy says. Anian hugs Mommy, but is still not sure about school.

After Mommy leaves, class starts with Ms. Maple telling the kids to put away their toys and come to the circle.

Ms. Grace and Anian head over to the circle. Anian sits down with the other students as Ms. Maple calls on each one to say their name and share their favorite thing to do. When she gets to Anian, she says, "Ok now, it's your turn Can you tell us your name and favorite thing to do?"

Anian looks around the room. He is still learning his words, so he uses signs and gestures when he speaks. He points to himself and says, "A!" Then he puffs his cheeks up and moves his arms like he's swimming.

The kids look at Anian and Ms. Maple, trying to figure out his favorite activity. All at once, they guess what it is and start shouting out, "Swimming!"

Anian gives a thumbs up to the class and says, "Yes!" Anian has the biggest smile as he looks around. School is getting better.

Ms. Maple says to the class, "Wonderful! Class, this is Anian, and he loves to swim."

As the day goes on, Anian learns along with the other students. Ms. Maple teaches everyone how to write letters, count numbers, and match colors.

Anian learns the same things as all the other students, just in different ways. To spell out his letters, he likes to use things he can touch, like sand or rice. To count his numbers, he likes to set out little toys in a row. And to work on his colors, he likes to sort colored blocks into their matching buckets.

During lunch, Anian sits with his class. He is having a good day, but he's starting to miss Mommy and Daddy. He is also feeling a bit shy as everyone talks and opens their lunch boxes.

Ms. Grace asks Anian if he needs help opening his lunch box. Ms. Grace is always happy to help Anian, but she also wants to make sure that he does some things by himself. It's important that Anian learns how to do some classroom activities all on his own.

Soon, a little boy scoots closer to Anian and says, "Hey, I'm Jamal. Do you want to be my friend?"

Anian looks at Jamal and says, "Yes!"

"Cool," says Jamal. "What do you have for lunch?"

Anian looks at his food. He picks up his drink and says, "Juice!"

Jamal smiles at Anian and helps him with the rest of his words. "Yep, you do have juice. And you have a sandwich, cookies, and ... Ooh my favorite: yogurt!"

Anian gives a thumbs up and the two friends eat lunch together.

For the rest of the day, Anian and Jamal learn and play together, with Ms. Grace looking on. Anian is doing great on his first day and has made a new friend!

All the children in the class love helping Anian, and Anian loves learning on his own too, just like everyone else.

The day goes by quickly and soon it's time to wrap up and get ready to go home.

When the last bell rings, Ms. Grace says, "Ok Anian, we are all done! You did it! You made it through your first day of school!"

Anian runs to get his book bag and is ready to go!

The children who are picked up by their parents all stand in line with one another. Ms. Grace stands with Anian so that they can head out together.

Jamal runs up and asks, "Can I walk with Anian? My parents are coming to get me, so we can walk together!"

"Sure," Ms. Grace says with a smile. Anian and Jamal walk ahead of Ms. Grace to the pick-up spot.

When they get to the pick-up spot, Anian sees Daddy and yells, "Da!" He runs toward Daddy, who scoops him up and gives him a big hug.

"Hey man," Daddy says. "I'm so happy to see you!"

Jamal runs up to them, (with Ms. Grace following close behind), and says, "Anian is my friend. We had a great day today!"

Daddy beams at Jamal and Anian. He says, "Anian, was school fun? Do you want to come back tomorrow?"

Anian puts his finger on his chin to think for a moment, then happily says, "Yes, again!" Then he gives Jamal a high five and says, "Bye-bye, J!"

Jamal smiles. "I really like that! I'm J and you're A. We're like superheroes with code names! Anian, we're going to be best friends!"

They all laugh and smile and wave goodbye to one another. Then Jamal leaves with his parents.

Daddy and Anian walk toward the car. "Anian, I'm so proud of you. You made it through the day and you made a new friend!"

"Yeah, J!" Anian says.

"How should we celebrate?" Daddy asks.

Anian stops walking and yells, "French fries and blue!" They laugh; it's their fun little secret. It's one of Anian's favorite things. French fries and blue it is!

They head toward the car to wait for Aven and Prix.

"Yay!" Anian says.

School isn't so scary after all!

CPSIA information can be obtained
at www.ICGtesting.com
Printed in the USA
BVHW061530100121
597441BV00004B/123